THE LAW OF TEACHER EVALUATION

A Self-Assessment Handbook

D0813710

by PERRY A. ZIRKEL

Published by the
Phi Delta Kappa Educational Foundation
in cooperation with the
National Organization on Legal Problems of Education

Cover design by Peg Caudell

This work was supported by the Office of Research,
Office of Educational Research and Improvement,
U.S. Department of Education (Grant No. R117Q00047).
The opinions expressed are those of the author,
and no official support by the U.S. Department of Education
is intended or should be inferred.

Library of Congress Catalog Card Number 96-67178
ISBN 0-87367-488-X
Copyright © 1996 by the Phi Delta Kappa Educational Foundation
Bloomington, Indiana U.S.A.

Table of Contents

Acknowledgements

I am grateful for the extensive research assistance of Susan Freeh, a doctoral student in educational leadership at Lehigh University, in compiling the overview of pertinent state legislation and regulations.

This publication was completed as part of a Center for Research on Educational Accountability and Teacher Evaluation (CREATE) project. CREATE is located in the Evaluation Center at Western Michigan University.

Introduction

The literature is replete with articles and monographs about the case law of teacher evaluation. The Resources section at the end of this book includes a useful sample of these. I use the term "teacher" in a generic sense, meaning professional personnel: classroom teachers, specialists, counselors, and, when applicable, administrators.

Unfortunately, such literature usually has two fundamental flaws. First, the authors seldom provide sufficient information about interrelated sources of law, such as state statutes and local collective bargaining agreements. For example, the best, relatively recent, comprehensive overview of state statutes is contained in an appendix to *Principles and Practices for Effective Teacher Evaluation* (1992) by Jerry W. Valentine. That overview does not list statutory citations; fails to differentiate among legislation, regulations, and state guidelines; includes teacher certification requirements where the state law legislated separate provisions for teacher evaluation; and indiscriminately mixes in statewide practices. However, these aspects were not part of the primary purpose of Valentine's book; his overview is an empirical survey of state education departments, rather than a direct analysis of statutes and regulations. No recent source gives useful attention to intersecting statutory issues, such as collective bargaining and open records; few address intersections with common law, such as defamation.

1

Second, the authors' legal interpretations and recommendations are colored by the norms of the education profession, and thus often fail to distinguish between the relevant law and lore.

The focus of this short book is on legal minimums, not professional optimums. My intention is to provide a summary resource that is current and comprehensive but also concise and coherent. For these reasons, I have based the information on an initial self-assessment for educators concerned with teacher evaluation. That self-assessment begins on the next page.

I advise readers of this volume to begin using this book by responding to the self-assessment. Answers and a detailed explanation for each item are provided in the section that follows the self-assessment. The explanations include extensive footnotes that cite pertinent court decisions. Following these explanations is a summary chart of relevant state statutes, regulations, and guidelines, again followed by specific citations.

This concise publication should be viewed as a starting point. For further information, I advise readers to consult the cited primary and secondary sources and to confer with competent counsel regarding specific issues in teacher evaluation.

Legal Boundaries for Teacher Evaluation: A Self-Assessment

Purchase of this book entitles the buyer to reproduce the self-assessment instrument that begins on the next page, without further permission, for use with students in college and university teacher education classes or for inservice staff development for education professionals.

Legal Boundaries for Teacher Evaluation: A Self-Assessment

DIRECTIONS: Circle the letter that represents your estimate of the current status of the national case law for each item. Use the following true-false scale:

A = Overwhelmingly false
B = Predominantly false
C = Virtually an even split
D = Predominantly true
E = Overwhelmingly true

Note: For a few of the items, the correct answer will be represented as a band, or range, comprising two adjacent response options. This results from incomplete congruence of the pertinent case law. The scope of the case law is national, but the framework is a mosaic of varying state statutes and regulations. Thus, for the accurate answers in an individual school district, it is essential to examine applicable state legislation, regulations, and guidelines as well as local policies and, where applicable, collective bargaining agreements in addition to pertinent case law.

Respond to the following 13 statements.

1. The use of teacher or student test scores is not legally permissible as a notable part of teacher evaluation that may lead to dismissal.
   [false]   A   B   C   D   E   [true]

2. Both evaluation procedures and criteria are mandatorily negotiable and arbitrable.
   [false]   A   B   C   D   E   [true]

3. Providing specific suggestions and extensive time for improvement is judicially required as an essential element of teacher evaluation that may lead to termination.
   [false]   A   B   C   D   E   [true]

4. Failure to strictly comply with state legislation and regulations specific to teacher evaluation will lead to defeat in court.
   [false]   A   B   C   D   E   [true]

5. Failure to strictly comply with local school board policies specifying procedures for teacher evaluation will lead to defeat in court.
   [false]   A   B   C   D   E   [true]

6. Courts will not uphold evaluations that are based on subjective criteria or data.
   [false]   A   B   C   D   E   [true]

7. Teachers face a high hurdle for proof when alleging discriminatory evaluation based on race, sex, or disability.
   [false]   A   B   C   D   E   [true]

8. Courts will not uphold dismissals based on evaluations that were affected by the outspokenness of the evaluated teacher.
   [false]   A   B   C   D   E   [true]

9. Videotaping a teacher for evaluation, without the teacher's permission or without providing a copy to the teacher prior to his or her termination hearing, violates the teacher's constitutional rights.
   [false]   A   B   C   D   E   [true]

10. School officials are wide open to liability for defamation if they communicate negative teacher evaluations to others as part of their responsibilities.
    [false]   A   B   C   D   E   [true]

11. Administrators who do not conduct proper evaluations are likely to suffer other costly consequences.
    [false]   A   B   C   D   E   [true]

12. Where an evaluated teacher fails to follow improvement directives, including attendance at review sessions, an incompetency case may become an insubordination case.
    [false]   A   B   C   D   E   [true]

13. Teacher performance evaluations are not subject to public disclosure under open records or freedom of information statutes.
    [false]   A   B   C   D   E   [true]

Answers and Explanations

1. The Use of Test Scores

Answer: B

Teacher Test Scores. A moderately long line of published court decisions are divided on the topic of teacher test scores. However, on balance, these decisions allow the use of such scores as a notable part of performance evaluation.

In a number of relatively early civil rights decisions, where the plaintiffs were minority group members, the courts rejected the use of the National Teacher Examination (NTE) as a prerequisite for a teaching certificate[1] and as the basis for nonrenewal[2] because of the lack of validation for these respective purposes. However, the courts generally allowed the NTE for differentiating salary levels, in light of their validation in relation to teacher training.[3] This split of judicial authority is close — in terms of court level and factual focus — with a slight trend toward more latitude for such testing. For example, toward the end of this period of civil rights litigation, a federal appeals court allowed the use of a teacher competency test as a requirement for admission into teacher education programs despite disparate racial results.[4] The controlling criterion of validity evidence stems from constitutional and statutory sources that are largely unavailing where the issue is not racial.

In a host of other decisions, the courts consistently have rejected a variety of challenges, such as breach of contract and substantive due process claims, to the use of competency tests for certifying or otherwise retaining teachers at the state[5] and local[6] levels.

Student Test Scores. A long, although not particularly thick, line of published court decisions rather consistently allows the use of student test scores at least as a notable part of nonrenewal[7] or termination.[8] Illustrative of the same judicial attitude, the West Virginia Supreme Court upheld the use of the students' grade distribution as part of the performance standards for a terminated teacher, even though this use was not expressly delineated in local board policy, and state regulations required "open and honest" evaluations.[9] The only exception was limited; a federal court denied dismissal of the certain due process claims of teachers challenging the use of standardized test scores as part of their evaluation process.[10] The final disposition of this claim was not published, but surviving a dismissal motion does not mean winning a judgment.

Conclusion. Thus, to a predominant but not overwhelming extent, the use of teacher or student test scores as a notable part of a performance-based dismissal decision is judicially permitted. No state prohibits such use by statute or regulation. However, one state (California), while mandating the use of student academic progress as a criterion, prohibits "the use of publishers' norms established by standardized tests" for the purpose of teacher evaluation.[11]

2. Negotiability and Arbitrability

Answer: A-B

Collective bargaining legislation applies to school districts in approximately two-thirds of the states. Among the most recent entries to the list are New Mexico and Ohio.[12] In states without applicable legislation, teacher-board negotiation is discretionary, except that the board may not bargain away nondelegable duties. At the same time, a few states — for example, North Carolina and Texas — expressly prohibit teacher-board bargaining.[13]

Where collective bargaining is required or permitted, the threshold issue is whether teacher evaluation is a negotiable issue. The

7

typical test is one of balancing the teachers' conditions of employment against the board's managerial prerogatives. The resulting categories are: 1) mandatory topics, which require good faith bargaining upon the initiation of either party; 2) permissive topics, which require good faith bargaining upon the initiation of either party; and 3) illegal topics, which are not enforceable in terms of either the process or product of bargaining.[14]

Where teacher evaluation is negotiable, the subsequent issue is whether it is arbitrable, that is, subject to enforceably binding grievance arbitration. The typical touchstone is the scope of the arbitration clause in the collective bargaining agreement.[15]

Negotiability. In the few states where teacher-based bargaining is prohibited altogether, or even where it is only voluntary, teacher evaluation is an illegal subject.[16] In the many states that have fully legislated teacher-board bargaining, a minority expressly establish teacher evaluation as a mandatory or permissive subject of bargaining; the majority of such statutes are silent on this issue.[17]

Where such legislation is silent, a few courts have concluded that teacher evaluation is a mandatory subject of negotiations.[18] However, the trend appears to be toward determining that teacher evaluation is either a permissive subject[19] or, more often, that only the procedures, not the criteria, of teacher evaluation are negotiable.[20]

Arbitrability. Inasmuch as arbitrability requires not only negotiability but also coverage by a contractual arbitration clause not in conflict with state school codes, teacher evaluation is arbitrable in even fewer cases. For example, in Iowa, where teacher evaluation is a mandatory topic for negotiations,[21] the state's highest court determined that performance evaluation was not arbitrable under the applicable language of a local collective bargaining agreement.[22] Another example is Illinois, where only teacher evaluation procedures, not criteria, are negotiable.[23] In that state, the courts concluded in two cases, based on the interacting coverage of state legislation and the local collective bar-

8

gaining agreement, that teacher evaluation grievances were not arbitrable.[24]

Thus the incidence of published court decisions in which teacher evaluation was determined to be arbitrable has been relatively low, largely limited to a few cases in New York (where, following the contours of negotiability, these cases were limited to procedural matters not precluded by state legislation)[25] and Pennsylvania.[26]

Conclusion. In sum, the current state of the case law across the various states is that 1) evaluation procedures are mandatorily negotiable in perhaps the majority of jurisdictions, but their arbitrability is more limited; and 2) evaluation criteria are rarely mandatory subjects of negotiation and arbitration. Conversely and more simply, the statement that both evaluation procedures and criteria are mandatorily negotiable and arbitrable is at least predominantly, probably overwhelmingly, false.

3. Remediation Plan and Probationary Period

Answer: C

As the statutory chart at the end of this book shows, specific suggestions and, to a less frequent extent, a substantial period for remediation are explicitly required by legislation or regulations in many, but far from all, jurisdictions. In these jurisdictions, the courts have invalidated teacher dismissals in several cases.[27] For example, West Virginia has been the scene of a consistent and continuing line of court decisions relying on regulatory requirements for remediation of both tenured and nontenured teachers.[28] Similarly, but not as strongly, the majority of the published remediation-related decisions in Illinois have favored the plaintiffs — teachers.[29]

However, judicial interpretation and enforcement of such statutory requirements have been less than vigorous, with notable erosion or limitations in such lines of case law. For example, in Illinois, a recent decision upheld the dismissal decision of a school district, holding that the plaintiff-teacher had no right to sue under the remediation statute where he had not exhausted available administrative procedures.[30] A more clear-cut example is an early pair of cases in Washington, where the appellate courts were rather relaxed in their enforcement of the remediation requirement, resulting in losses for the teacher-plaintiffs.[31] Similarly, the clear majority of relevant court decisions in Missouri have provided winning latitude to school boards.[32] One does not have to look far, particularly in recent times, for other examples of less than rigorous judicial interpretation of statutory remediation requirements, with the outcome being adverse to the plaintiff-teacher.[33]

More often than not, in jurisdictions where there is not an express requirement in state law, the courts have turned deaf ears on the plaintiff-teacher's argument that specific suggestions and substantial time for improvement are implicitly part of reasonable, good-faith personnel actions. Unless the gap is filled by an express requirement in a local collective bargaining agreement,[34] the modern case law has, with an occasional exception, refused to impose such requirements.[35] For example, Wyoming's highest court upheld the dismissal of a nontenured teacher for incompetence even though the school board failed to follow its own policy that required annual written evaluations and a probationary period.[36]

Conclusion. On balance, considering both the states that require by legislation or regulation specific prescriptions and a substantial period for improvement and those that do not, the statement that they have been judicially required is relatively evenly split.

4. Noncompliance with State Law

Answer: C

Reflecting the same trend of item 3 on a broader basis, the courts have been less than expansive in applying requirements of state teacher evaluation statutes and regulations. The relevant court decisions are divisible into those cases where the issue was substantive, such as whether an unsatisfactory evaluation was supported by sufficient evidence, and those where the issue was procedural, such as whether a discharge is warranted where the school administration failed to support an unsatisfactory evaluation with anecdotal records as required by state regulations.

Substantive Matters. Adhering to a long tradition of "academic abstention," the courts' deference to school districts' adverse actions, such as nonrenewal[37] and termination,[38] has been strong in substantive issues arising from performance evaluation, such as whether the evaluator has sufficient subject matter expertise or whether conflicting evidence, on balance, favors the resulting adverse action. The exceptions in such evidentiary matters have been relatively rare.[39] In two such cases, the courts reversed terminations of teachers for incompetence where their overall evaluation ratings were satisfactory.[40]

Procedural Matters. In general, the courts have been notably less deferential to school boards in procedural than in substantive matters. For example, the courts generally have rejected nonrenewal of nontenured teachers where school boards have failed to provide statutorily required procedural due process.[41] However, though the specifically relevant case law reveals that failure to follow the procedural requirements of state teacher evaluation statutes and regulations may be ill-advised,[42] a recently lengthening line of exceptions counterbalances the traditional trend.[43] For example, in Ohio, where legislation requires written notice to the teacher of specific recommendations and means of assistance, the state's highest court upheld the nonrenewal of a nontenured teacher despite the school district's failure to meet this procedural requirement in the first evaluation report. In a relaxed rather than strict interpretation, the court considered the required recommendations and supervisory assistance incorporated by reference in the second evaluation report.[44]

Conclusion. Failure to strictly comply with state legislation and regulations specific to teacher evaluation does not necessarily mean that the district will lose the case. Viewing compliance as primarily a procedural matter, with substantive matters being in the background, the relevant case law, particularly in recent years, is relatively balanced between precedents favoring teachers and those favoring school boards.

5. Noncompliance with Local Policies

Answer: B-C

The courts have been less than strict where school districts have failed to follow the procedural specifications of their own evaluation policies. The court decisions that have favored plaintiff-teachers in such circumstances[45] have been more than matched by the case law in favor of the defendant-districts.[46] However, most of the court decisions in favor of the defendant-districts were affected by the nontenured status of the teacher or by the procedural posture of the case, such as an intervening ruling by the state board of education. Thus the answer for this item is either predominantly false or virtually an even split.

6. Subjective Criteria and Data

Answer: A

The case law pertaining to subjective criteria and data for teacher evaluation is more limited than that pertaining to the previous pair of items. Rather than being split, however, these court decisions have been quite consistent in upholding personnel actions based on subjective criteria and data.[47] For example, even where a state statute for career ladder advancement required "objective" evaluation, an appeals court upheld a denial based on professional judgment in the absence of preponderant proof of bias or prejudice.[48]

One might expect an expansive exception where the teacher is a member of a minority group, triggering the more strict scrutiny of constitutional and statutory civil rights protection. However, as exemplified by a decision by a federal court of appeals,[49] subjective evaluations are not precluded by such scrutiny. Thus the generalization that courts will not uphold evaluations that are based on subjective criteria or data is overwhelmingly, if not totally, contradicted by the pertinent case law.

7. Race, Sex, or Disability Discrimination

Answer: D-E

Overlapping with the aforementioned examples of relevant litigation, defendant-districts theoretically are subject to closer judicial scrutiny when the plaintiff-teacher is entitled to special constitutional or statutory antidiscrimination protection. Specifically, the applicable constitutional provision is the Fourteenth Amendment equal protection clause. When applied to race-based claims, the courts have accorded "strict scrutiny" to governmental decisions. Under this level of scrutiny, school districts and other government agencies must show a compelling, rather than merely rational, justification. Fourteenth Amendment claims based on gender and disability have generally not received the same strict level of scrutiny. The primarily applicable legislation, which has accompanying federal regulations, for race-based claims is Title VII of the Civil Rights Act, also known as the Equal Employment Opportunities Act. Gender-based claims also are covered by Title VII, as well as by Title IX. However, the corresponding protection for disability is found in Section 504 of the Rehabilitation Act and the Americans with Disabilities Act.

In practice, the plaintiff-teacher faces a daunting problem of proof. Although in the early court decisions, arising within the especially sensitive context of desegregation, African-American teachers succeeded in proving that personnel actions based on performance evaluations were discriminatory in violation of federal law,[50] the recent record has been barren.[51] Although not yet yielding published court decisions specifically targeting performance evaluation, teachers have evidenced steep uphill, parallel proof problems in related litigation based on gender[52] and disability.[53]

Conclusion. Pertinent civil rights case law reveals to a predominant or even overwhelming extent that teachers face a high hurdle for proving claims of discriminatory evaluation based on race, sex, or disability.[54]

8. Outspoken Evaluatees

Answer: B

Civil rights claims extend beyond discrimination, based on the Fourteenth Amendment or its implementing legislation, to include expression, based on the First Amendment. The Supreme Court has established the following three-step test for First Amendment expression claims.[55]

I. The plaintiff-teacher has the burden of proving that his or her expression concerned a public issue and, if so, that his or her right of expression concerning public issues outweighed the defendant-district's obligation to operate an effective system.

II. If he or she prevails on Step I, the plaintiff-teacher has the burden of also proving that his or her expression was a substantial factor in causing the adverse personnel action.

III. If the plaintiff-teacher prevails on Steps I and II, the burden shifts to the defendant-district to prove that it would have taken the adverse action regardless of the teacher's expression.

Thus far, the proportion of the pertinent published court decisions in which the plaintiff-teachers have succeeded in passing this three-step test is clearly the minority.[56] Faced with these successive hurdles, plaintiff-teachers have failed variously at all steps: I,[57] II,[58] and III.[59]

Conclusion. Based on the judicial formulation and application of the criteria for First Amendment expression, the odds of an outspoken teacher-evaluatee succeeding on such a constitutional claim are predominantly, although not overwhelmingly, unfavorable.

9. Videotaping

Answer: A-B

The relatively recent use of videotaping for teacher evaluation has led to only a couple of pertinent published court decisions thus far. In the most noteworthy of these, a Texas appeals court upheld the termination of a teacher, ruling that the school district's involuntary videotaping of her performance did not violate her right of privacy and that the district's failure to provide her with a copy of the tape prior to the hearing did not violate her due process rights.[60] Another case was only partially on the point, but the outcome revealed a similar judicial stance. In this case, Missouri's highest court upheld the termination of a teacher based in part on self-videotaping, which was required for the purpose of professional development but which was not accompanied by a warning of possible use for the purpose of dismissal.[61]

When viewed within these limits, the published case law to date is overwhelmingly permissive of videotaping for performance evaluation; however, when viewed in comparison to the case law specific to the other items in this self-assessment, its limited weight justifies the alternate, "predominant" answer.

10. Defamation

Answer: A

Illustrating the intersection with common law, rather than constitutional law, the issue is the extent to which teacher evaluation can lead to liability for defamation. Termed "slander" in its oral form and "libel" in its written form, defamation generally requires a judgment that communication to one or more third parties stigmatized the plaintiff's reputation in the community. Although they share a basic template, the states have variations on the common law theme of defamation. For example, in some states falsity is an essential element of defamation, while in others truth is an effective defense against an action alleging defamation.

The immunity defense is applicable to a school board member's or administrator's communications of negative evaluations. In some states, school board members and administrators, at least the superintendent, have an absolute immunity in defamation cases arising within the scope of their duties. In such states, the defamation claims of plaintiff-teachers in performance evaluation cases have failed.[62] In other states, administrators have a qualified immunity, providing an effective defense within their scope of employment unless the plaintiff proves malice. In such states, the relevant cases have been decided largely in favor of the defendant-administrators with only partial exceptions.[63]

Exemplifying the partial exceptions, the appeals court in a Michigan case remanded for trial whether the superintendent acted with actual malice in sending negative evaluation letters about the plaintiff-principal to the school board.[64] The only other partial exception to date has been a decision in which the appellate court remanded the plaintiff's defamation claim to the trial court to determine whether the defendant-board members were acting within the scope of their duties.[65]

The conclusion that school officials are likely to be liable for defamation for communicating negative evaluations to others as part of their responsibilities is overwhelmingly false.

11. Other Costly Consequences

Answer: B

Administrators who do not conduct proper evaluations, in conformity with the applicable legal rights and duties, may suffer two other primary forms of adverse consequences: discipline, including discharge, and liability, extending beyond defamation claims.

Discipline/Discharge. The number of pertinent published decisions has been limited, but their outcomes have been consistent. In two separate cases, appellate courts have upheld the termination of principals who failed to develop and implement evaluation of teachers in accordance with school board policies.[66] However, in each case, there was at least one other performance problem by the principal.

Liability. In addition to the aforementioned defamation cases, other suits by teachers arising from allegedly improper performance evaluations also have been largely unsuccessful. In one case, a Michigan appellate court rejected claims of negligence, civil conspiracy, and intentional infliction of mental distress arising from an unsatisfactory rating.[67] Similarly, in another relevant case, a Missouri appeals court rejected claims of breach of contract and interference with contractual relations.[68] However, in the third pertinent decision, Alabama's highest court denied a motion to dismiss a teacher's breach of contract claim premised on the school district's alleged failure to follow its adopted teacher evaluation policy.[69]

In light of the limited amount and mixed nature of the pertinent case law, the appropriate answer to the "other costly consequences" item appears to be predominantly false.

12. Insubordination

Answer: E

Although the typical performance evaluation case is based on incompetency, the grounds may shift additionally or alternatively to insubordination if the teacher fails to follow reasonable evaluation-related directives. Published court decisions provide clear and consistent examples of teacher-evaluatees who have been defensibly dismissed for failing to attend administrative conferences or failing to implement suggestions for improvement.[70] Thus the answer to this item is overwhelmingly true.

13. Open Records Legislation

Answer: B-C

Several states have open records or freedom of information statutes that provide public access to certain government documents. The recorded performance evaluations of public school teachers are subject to public disclosure under some statutes. On the other hand, a clear minority of states, including Alaska, California, and Connecticut, expressly exclude performance evaluation records from open records statutes.

Where the open records statutes do not expressly exclude performance evaluations and thus are ambiguous, the balance appears to weigh closely in favor of disclosure. In arguably analogous litigation, appellate courts have held that teachers' grievance records,[71] attendance records,[72] college transcripts,[73] personnel files,[74] confidential settlement,[75] and other recorded information[76] were subject to disclosure under such statutes.

In one of the few cases directly concerned with this issue, Connecticut's highest court held that teacher performance documents are — depending on the discretion of the state Freedom of Information Commission — subject to disclosure.[77]

An appeals court in the state of Washington similarly interpreted the ambiguity in favor of releasing a teacher's performance evaluations.[78] However, the state legislature changed the statute soon after to eliminate the ambiguity. Subsequently, in another case, the same appellate court rejected disclosure of a principal's performance evaluations.[79] Similarly, a New York appellate court ruled that a teacher's performance documents were "squarely" excluded by the relevant state legislation.[80]

Thus, on balance, the generalization that, where states have such open records statutes, teacher performance evaluations are not subject to disclosure appears to be predominantly false or an even split.

Overall Conclusion

The legal boundaries for performance evaluation of professional educators in the public schools, especially those drawn by courts in the substantial spaces left open by state statutes and regulations, are much broader than are realized by the typical evaluator or evaluatee. Both often confuse the pertinent law with the professional lore. Rather than feeling fearful of or hamstrung by the rulings of federal and state courts, school officials should focus on doing the "right thing" — based on professional norms — in local agreements, policies, and practices. As a starting point, it is worthwhile to check the applicable framework of legislation, regulations, and case law in individual jurisdictions. In all likelihood, school personnel — both those who evaluate and those who are evaluated — will find ample legal latitude in designing and conducting personnel evaluation for both positive and negative career consequences.

Notes on Answers and Explanations

1. Georgia Ass'n of Educators, Inc. v. Nix, 407 F. Supp. 1102 (N.D. Ga. 1976); *cf.* Baker v. Columbus Municipal Separate Sch. Dist., 462 F.2d 1112 (5th Cir. 1972); Armstead v. Municipal Separate Sch. Dist., 461 F.2d 276 (5th Cir. 1972).
2. York v. Alabama State Bd. of Educ., 581 F. Supp. 779 (M.D. Ala. 1983); *cf.* Allen v. Alabama State Bd. of Educ., 816 F.2d 575 (11th Cir. 1987).
3. United States v. South Carolina, 434 U.S. 1026 (1978); Newman v. Crews, 651 F.2d 222 (4th Cir. 1981); *cf.* Moore v. Tangipahoa Parish Sch. Bd., 594 F.2d 489 (5th Cir. 1979).
4. United States v. LULAC, 793 F.2d 636 (5th Cir. 1986).
5. Fields v. Hallsville Indep. Sch. Dist., 906 F.2d 1017 (5th Cir. 1990); State v. Project Principle, Inc., 724 S.W.2d 387 (Tex. 1987); Texas State Bd. of Educ. v. Guffy, 718 S.W.2d 48 (Tex. 1986); Texas State Teachers Ass'n v. State, 711 S.W.2d 421 (Tex. Ct. App. 1986); *cf.* Harris v. National Evaluation Sys., Inc., 719 F. Supp. 1081 (N.D. Ga. 1989).
6. Alba v. Los Angeles Unified Sch. Dist., 189 Cal. Rptr. 897 (Ct. App. 1983).
7. Scheelhaase v. Woodbury Cent. Sch. Dist., 488 F.2d 237 (8th Cir. 1973), *cert. denied*, 417 U.S. 969 (1974).
8. In re Termination of Johnson, 451 N.W.2d 343 (Minn. Ct. App. 1990); *cf.* Fay v. Board of Directors, 298 N.W.2d 345 (Iowa 1980); Whaley v. Anoka-Hennepin Indep. Sch. Dist., 325 N.W.2d 128 (Minn. 1982). Conversely, illustrating the latitude for school board discretion, a state appellate court upheld the termination of a

20

teacher based on unsatisfactory performance despite improvement in the students' standardized test scores. Johnson v. Francis Howell R-3 Bd. of Educ., 868 S.W.2d 191 (Mo. Ct. App. 1994).

9. Brown v. Wood County Bd. of Educ., 400 S.E.2d 213 (W. Va. 1990).

10. St. Louis Teachers Union v. Bd. of Educ., 652 F. Supp. 425 (E.D. Mo. 1987). The court denied the defendant district's motion to dismiss the teachers' procedural, based on property (salary advancement), and substantive due process claims. At the same time, the court granted the defendant district's motion to dismiss their other Fourteenth Amendment claims, which were based on equal protection as well as due process.

11. CAL. EDUC. CODE §44662.

12. *See, e.g.*, James A. Rapp, *Education Law, vol. 4* (New York: Matthew Bender, 1993), Table 11.

13. *See., e.g.*, Perry Zirkel, "RIF and Collective Bargaining," *West's Education Law Reporter* 95 (1995): 31-47.

14. *Id.*, p. 32.

15. *Id.* p. 36.

16. In Louisiana, for example, teacher negotiations are permissive, but teacher evaluation is a prohibited subject. *See* United Teachers v. Orleans Parish Sch. Bd., 340 So.2d 232 (La. Ct. App. 1977).

17. *See, e.g.*, Kirsten Zerger, "Teacher Evaluation and Collective Bargaining: A Union Perspective," *Journal of Law & Education* 17 (1988): 511.

18. *See, e.g.*, Evansville-Vanderburgh Sch. Corp. v. Roberts, 405 N.E.2d 895 (Ind. 1980); Board of Sch. Trustees v. Indiana Educ. Employment Relations Bd., 543 N.E.2d 662 (Ind. Ct. App. 1989); Northeast Community Sch. Dist. v. Public Employment Relations Bd., 408 N.W.2d 46 (Iowa 1987); Aplington Community Sch. Dist. v. Iowa Pub. Employment Relations Bd., 392 N.W.2d 495 (Iowa 1986); *cf.* Central Michigan Univ. Faculty Ass'n v. Central Michigan Univ., 273 N.W.2d 21 (Mich. 1978). In addition, see the entries in the Comments column of the Summary Chart on pages 32-33 for those states, such as Indiana, Massachusetts, Minnesota, and Rhode Island, where the state legislation for teacher evaluation expressly requires collective bargaining.

19. *See, e.g.*, Springfield Educ. Ass'n v. Springfield Sch. Dist., 621 P.2d 547 (Or. 1980); Milberry v. Board of Educ., 354 A.2d 559 (Pa.

1976); *cf.* Wethersfield Bd. of Educ. v. Connecticut Bd. of Labor Relations, 519 A.2d 41 (Conn. 1986) (not mandatory). In addition, see the Summary Chart for those states, such as Nevada, New York, and Oklahoma, where the relevant state legislation requires consultation with collective bargaining or other teachers' representatives.

20. *See, e.g.,* Alton Community Sch. Dist. v. Illinois Educ. Labor Relations Bd., 567 N.E.2d 671 (Ill. App. Ct. 1992); Board of Educ. v. NEA-Goodland, 785 P.2d 993 (Kan. 1990); Bethlehem Township Bd. of Educ. v. Bethlehem Township Educ. Ass'n, 449 A.2d 1254 (N.J. 1982); *cf.* School Comm. v. Korbut, 358 N.E.2d 831 (Mass. App. Ct. 1976); Fargo Educ. Ass'n v. Fargo Pub. Sch. Dist., 291 N.W.2d 267 (N.D. 1980); Board of Educ. v. Newburgh Teachers Ass'n, 537 N.Y.S.2d 250 (App. Div. 1989); Beloit Educ. Ass'n v. Wisconsin Employment Relations Bd., 242 N.W.2d 231 (Wis. 1976).

21. Northeast Community Sch. Dist. v. Public Employment Relations Bd., 408 N.W.2d 46 (Iowa 1987); Aplington Community Sch. Dist. v. Iowa Pub. Employment Relations Bd., 392 N.W.2d 495 (Iowa 1986).

22. Atlantic Educ. Ass'n v. School Dist., 469 N.W.2d 689 (Iowa 1991).

23. Alton Community Sch. Dist. v. Illinois Educ. Labor Relations Bd., 567 N.E.2d 671 (Ill. App. Ct. 1992) (inconsistent with state dismissal statute). However, the effect of this ruling is subject to possible change depending on the outcome of an intervening remand to the IELRB for application of a three-part balancing test. Board of Educ. v. Illinois Educ. Relations Bd, 556 N.E.2d 857 (Ill. App. Ct. 1990), *modified and remanded,* 599 N.E.2d 892 (Ill. 1992).

24. Board of Educ. v. Illinois Educ. Labor Relations Bd., 629 N.E.2d 797 (Ill. App. Ct. 1994); Board of Educ. v. Illinois Educ. Labor Relations Bd., 617 N.E.2d 790 (Ill. App. Ct. 1993) (not collectively bargained). For similar examples in New Jersey, see Board of Educ. v. Fairlawn Educ. Ass'n, 417 A.2d 76 (N.J. Super. Ct. App. Div. 1980); In re Teaneck Bd. of Educ., 390 A.2d 1191 (N.J. Super. Ct. App. Div. 1978)

25. Riverhead Cent. Sch. Dist. v. Faculty Ass'n, 531 N.Y.S.2d 658 (1988); Clarkstown Cent. Sch. Dist. v. Cacciola, 558 N.Y.S.2d 704 (App. Div. 1990).

26. Milberry v. Board of Educ., 354 A.2d 559 (Pa. 1976); Mifflin County Sch. Dist. v. Lutz, 551 A.2d 396 (Pa. Commw. Ct. 1988);

Oxford Bd. of School Directors v. Pennsylvania Labor Relations Bd., 376 A.2d 1012 (Pa. Commw. Ct. 1977). Additionally, in a California case, the court upheld arbitrability but restricted the arbitrator's remedial authority. Bellflower Educ. Ass'n v. Bellflower Unified Sch. Dist., 279 Cal. Rptr. 179 (Ct. App. 1991).

27. *See, e.g.,* Gunter v. Board of Trustees, 854 P.2d 253 (Idaho 1993); Board of Sch. Directors v. Merrymaking Educ. Ass'n, 354 A.2d 169 (Me. 1976); Ganyo v. Independent Sch. Dist., 311 N.W.2d 497 (Minn. 1981); *cf.* Munger v. Jesup Community Sch. Dist., 325 N.W.2d 377 (Iowa 1982). In some of the cases, however, the court concluded that the district met the remediation requirements. *See. e.g.,* Childers v. Independent Sch. Dist. No. 1, 645 P.2d 992 (Okla. 1981); *cf.* McKenzie v. Webster Parish Sch. Bd., 609 So.2d 1028 (La. Ct. App. 1992) (reserved for trial). The plaintiff was non-tenured in some of these cases and tenured in others, depending on the statutory coverage.

28. Hosaflook v. Nestor, 346 S.E.2d 798 (W. Va. 1986); Wren v. McDowell Bd. of Educ., 327 S.E.2d 464 (W. Va. 1985); Holland v. Board of Educ., 327 S.E.2d 155 (W. Va. 1985); Lipan v. Board of Educ., 295 S.E.2d 44 (W. Va. 1982); Wilt v. Flanigan, 294 S.E.2d 189 (W. Va. 1982); Mason County Bd. of Educ. v. State Superintendent of Sch., 274 S.E.2d 435 (W. Va. 1980).

29. Morris v. Board of Educ., 421 N.E.2d 387 (Ill. App. Ct. 1981); Board of Educ. v. Illinois State Bd. of Educ., 403 N.E.2d 277 (Ill. App. Ct. 1980). *But see* Community Unit Sch. Dist. v. Maclin, 435 N.E.2d 845 (Ill. App. Ct. 1982); *cf.* Powell v. Board of Educ., 545 N.E.2d 767 (Ill. App. Ct. 1989).

30. Dudley v. Board of Educ., 632 N.E.2d 94 (Ill. App. Ct. 1994).

31. Sargent v. Selah Sch. Dist., 599 P.2d 25 (Wash. Ct. App. 1979); Van Horn v. Highline Sch. Dist., 562 P.2d 641 (Wash. Ct. App. 1977).

32. *Compare* Johnson v. Francis Howell R-3 Bd. of Educ., 868 S.W. 2d 191 (Mo. 1993); O'Connell v. School District, 830 S.W. 2d 410 (Mo. 1992); Newcomb v. Humansville R-IV Sch. Dist., 908 S.W. 2d 821 (Mo. Ct. App. 1995); Keesee Meadow Heights R-II Sch. Dist., 865 S.W.2d 818 (Mo. Ct. App. 1993); Cozad v. Crane Sch. Dist. R-3, 716 S.W.2d 408 (Mo. Ct. App. 1986); Hanlon v. Board of Educ., 695 S.W.2d 930 (Mo. Ct. App. 1985) *with* Selby v. North Callway Bd. of Educ., 777 S.W.2d 275 (Mo. Ct. App. 1989); Iven

v. Hazelwood Sch. Dist., 710 S.W.2d 462 (Mo. Ct. App. 1986). The plaintiff-teachers in all of these cases were tenured, reflecting the preferential protection for them in Missouri relating to remediation.

33. *See, e.g.*, Gaulden v. Lincoln Parish Sch. Bd., 554 So.2d 152 (La. Ct. App. 1989); Rickel v. Cloverleaf Local Sch. Dist., 608 N.E.2d 767 (Ohio Ct. App. 1992); In re Termination of Johnson, 451 N.W.2d 343 (Minn. Ct. App. 1990); Schofield v. Richland County Sch. Dist., 447 S.E.2d 189 (S.C. 1994). *But cf.* Brown v. Caldwell Sch. Dist., 898 P.2d 43 (Idaho 1995). The plaintiff teachers in these cases varied with respect to being nontenured or tenured.

34. *See, e.g.,* Paramount Unified Sch. Dist. v. Teachers Ass'n of Paramount, 32 Cal. Rptr.2d 311 (Ct. App. 1994).

35. *See, e.g.,* Miller v. Board of Educ., 752 P.2d 113 (Kan. 1988); Trustees v. Spivey, 866 P.2d 208 (Mont. 1993); Nordhagen v. Hot Springs Sch. Dist., 474 N.W.2d 510 (S.D. 1991); *cf.* Halm v. Board of Educ., 436 N.W.2d 680 (Mich. Ct. App. 1988). *But see* Perron v. Royal Oak Sch. Dist., 400 N.W.2d 709 (Mich. Ct. App. 1986). The plaintiffs' tenure status did not seem to be controlling in these cases.

36. Leonard v. Converse County Sch. Dist., 788 P.2d 1119 (Wyo. 1990).

37. *See, e.g.*, Beauchamp v. Davis, 550 F.2d 959 (4th Cir. 1977); Wilson v. Des Moines Indep. Community Sch. Dist., 389 N.W.2d 681 (Iowa Ct. App. 1986); Jennings v. Caddo Parish Sch. Bd., 276 So.2d 386 (La. Ct. App. 1973); Phillis v. Board of Sch. Directors, 617 A.2d 830 (Pa. Commw. Ct. 1992); Homan v. Blue Ridge Sch. Dist., 405 A.2d 572 (Pa. Commw. Ct. 1979); Busker v. Board of Educ., 295 N.W.2d 1 (S.D. 1980).

38. *See, e.g.*, Pratt v. Alabama State Tenure Comm'n, 394 So.2d 18 (Ala. Civ. App. 1980), *cert. denied,* 394 So.2d 22 (Ala. 1981); DeBernard v. State Bd. of Educ., 527 N.E.2d 616 (Ill. App. Ct. 1988); Stamper v. Board of Educ., 491 N.E.2d 36 (Ill. App. Ct. 1986); Harrison-Washington Community Sch. Corp. v. Bales, 450 N.E.2d 559 (Ind. Ct. App. 1983); Fay v. Board of Directors, 298 N.W.2d 345 (Iowa 1980); Board of Directors v. Mroz, 295 N.W.2d 447 (Iowa 1980); Briggs v. Board of Directors, 282 N.W.2d 740 (Iowa 1979); Rainwater v. Board of Educ., 645 S.W.2d 172 (Mo. 1982); Atherton v. Board of Educ., 744 S.W.2d 518 (Mo. Ct. App.

1988); Hanlon v. Board of Educ., 695 S.W.2d 930 (Mo. Ct. App. 1985); Donnes v. State, 672 P.2d 617 (Mont. 1983); Eshom v. Board of Educ., 364 N.W.2d 7 (Neb. 1985); Crump v. Durham County Bd. of Educ., 327 S.E.2d 599 (N.C. Ct. App. 1985); Davidson v. Winston-Salem/Forsyth County Bd. of Educ., 303 S.E.2d 202 (N.C. Ct. App. 1983); Mongitore v. Regan, 520 N.Y.S.2d 194 (App. Div. 1987), *app. denied,* 526 N.Y.S.2d 436 (1988); Faville v. Ambach, 507 N.Y.S.2d 310 (App. Div. 1986), *app. denied,* 517 N.Y.S.2d 1026 (1987); Clarke v. Board of Educ., 482 N.Y.S.2d 80 (App. Div. 1984); Grant v. Board of Sch. Directors, 471 A.2d 1292 (Pa. Commw. Ct. 1984); Kudasik v. Board of Sch. Directors, 455 A.2d 261 (Pa. Commw. Ct. 1983); Sanders v. Anderson, 746 S.W.2d 185 (Tenn. 1987).

39. *See, e.g.,* Hollingsworth v. Board of Educ., 303 N.W.2d 506 (Neb. 1981); Sanders v. Board of Educ., 263 N.W.2d 461 (Neb. 1978); Williams v. Pittard, 604 S.W.2d 845 (Tenn. 1980).

40. *See, e.g.,* Trustees v. Anderson, 757 P.2d 1315 (Mont. 1988); Schulz v. Board of Educ., 315 N.W.2d 633 (Neb. 1982).

41. *See, e.g.,* Orth v. Phoenix Union High Sch. System, 613 P.2d 311 (Ariz. Ct. App. 1980); Witgenstein v. School Bd., 347 So.2d 1069 (Fla. Dist. Ct. App. 1977); Kruse v. Board of Directors, 231 N.W.2d 626 (Iowa 1973); Seifert v. Lingleville Indep. Sch. Dist., 692 S.W.2d 461 (Tex. 1985).

42 *See, e.g.,* Gilliland v. Board of Educ., 343 N.E.2d 704 (Ill. App. Ct. 1976); Lehman v. Board of Educ., 439 N.Y.S.2d 670 (App. Div. 1981); Carter v. Craig, 574 S.W.2d 352 (Ky. Ct. App. 1978); Farmer v. Kelleys Island Bd. of Educ., 630 N.E.2d 721 (Ohio 1994); Hosler v. Bellefonte Area Sch. Dist., 395 A.2d 289 (Pa. Commw. Ct. 1977); George v. Union Area Sch. Dist., 350 A.2d 918 (Pa. Commw. Ct. 1976); Hyde v. Wellpinit Sch. Dist., 611 P.2d 1388 (Wash. Ct. App. 1980).

43. *See, e.g.,* Gibson v. City of Cranston, 37 F.3d 731 (1st Cir. 1994); Goodrich v. Newport News Sch. Bd., 743 F.2d 225 (4th Cir. 1984); Lamar Sch. Dist. No. 39 v. Kinder, 642 S.W.2d 885 (Ark. 1985); California Teachers Ass'n v. Governing Bd., 192 Cal. Rptr. 358 (Ct. App. 1982), *cert. denied sub nom Takahashi v. Governing Bd.,* 465 U.S. 1008 (1983); Krischer v. School Bd., 555 So.2d 436 (Fla. 1990); Moran v. Board of Sch. Trustees, 501 N.E.2d 472 (Ind. Ct.

App. 1986); Randall v. Community Sch. Dist., 528 N.W.2d 588 (Iowa 1995); O'Connell v. School Dist., 830 S.W.2d 410 (Mo. 1992); Nevels v. Board of Educ., 822 S.W.2d 898 (Mo. Ct. App. 1991); Adkins v. Hazelwood Sch. Dist., 743 S.W.2d 869 (Mo. Ct. App. 1987); Clinton v. Wake County Bd. of Educ., 424 S.E.2d 691 (N.C. 1993); Dore v. Board of Educ., 449 A.2d 547 (N.J. Super. Ct. 1982); State ex rel. Martines v. Cleveland City Sch. Dist. Bd. of Educ., 639 N.E.2d 80 (Ohio 1994); Borman v. Gorham-Fayette Bd. of Educ., 502 N.E.2d 1031 (Ohio 1986); Vorm v. David Douglas Sch. Dist., 608 P.2d 193 (Or. 1980); Board of Educ. v. Kushner, 530 A.2d 541 (Pa. Commw. Ct. 1987); Hamburg v. North Penn Sch. Dist., 484 A.2d 867 (Pa. Commw. Ct. 1984); Board of Pub. Instruction v. Pyle, 390 A.2d 904 (Pa. Commw. Ct. 1978); Schaub v. Chamberlain Bd. of Educ., 339 N.W.2d 307 (S.D. 1983); Roberts v. Lincoln County Sch. Dist., 676 P.2d 577 (Wyo. 1984); *cf.* Dunson v. Alabama State Tenure Comm'n, 653 So.2d 998 (Ala. Civ. Ct. App. 1995); Jefferson v. Compton Unified Sch. Dist., 17 Cal. Rptr. 2d 474 (Ct. App. 1993); Burk v. Unified Sch. Dist., 646 F. Supp. 1557 (D. Kan. 1986); Berhorst v. Maries County R-II Sch. Dist., 805 S.W.2d 696 (Mo. Ct. App. 1991); Haywood v. State Bd. of Educ., 874 S.W.2d 67 (Tenn. Ct. App. 1993); Amarillo Indep. Sch. Dist. v. Meno, 854 S.W.2d 950 (Tex. Ct. App. 1993).

44. Thomas v. Board of Educ., 643 N.E.2d 131 (Ohio 1994).

45. *See, e.g.,* Board of Educ. v. Ballard, 507 A.2d 192 (Md. Ct. Spec. App. 1986); Longarzo v. Anker, 373 N.Y.S.2d 199 (App. Div. 1975); *cf.* Maxwell v. Southside School Dist., 618 S.W.2d 148 (Ark. 1981) (hearing procedures).

46. *See, e.g.,* Longarzo v. Anker, 578 F.2d 469 (2d Cir. 1978); Willis v. Widefield Sch. Dist., 603 P.2d 962 (Colo. Ct. App. 1977); McKenzie v. Webster Parish Sch. Bd., 653 So.2d 215 (La. Ct. App. 1995); Marotta v. Greater New Bedford Regional Vo-Tech. High Sch. Comm., 589 N.E.2d 334 (Mass. App. Ct. 1992); Board of Sch. Comm'rs v. Davis, 625 A.2d 361 (Md. Ct. Spec. App. 1993); Leonard v. Converse County Sch. Dist., 788 P.2d 1119 (Wyo. 1990); *cf.* Barnett v. Board of Educ., 654 A.2d 720 (Conn. 1995) (arbitration); Board of Educ. v. Barbano, 411 A.2d 124 (Md. Ct. Spec. App. 1980) (state policies); Shapiro v. School Dist., 637 A.2d 718 (Pa. Commw. Ct. 1994) (arbitration). Conversely, where a

board complied with its evaluation procedures and obtained favorable ratings for a nontenured teacher, the court refused to infer a right to her renewal. King v. Jefferson County Bd. of Educ., 659 So.2d 686 (Ala. Cir. Ct. App. 1995).

47. *See, e.g.*, Rogers v. Department of Defense Dependent Sch., 814 F.2d 1549 (Fed. Cir. 1987); Perez v. Commission on Professional Competence, 197 Cal. Rptr. 390 (Ct. App. 1983); Trustees v. Spivey, 866 P.2d 208 (Mont. 1993); Schneider v. McLaughlin Indep. Sch. Dist., 241 N.W.2d 574 (S.D. 1976); Higgins v. Board of Educ., 286 S.E.2d 682 (W. Va. 1987); *cf.* Mackey v. Newell-Providence Community Sch. Dist., 412 S.E.2d 5 (Iowa Ct. App. 1992); Spry v. Winston-Salem/Forsyth County Bd. of Educ., 483 N.W.2d 687 (N.C. 1992); Iversen v. Wall Bd. of Educ., 522 N.W.2d 188 (S.D. 1994).

48. Sallee v. State Bd. of Educ., 828 S.W.2d 742 (Tenn. Ct. App. 1992).

49. Tyler v. Hot Springs Sch. Dist., 827 F.2d 1227 (8th Cir. 1987). For further such court decisions, see *infra* note 51 and accompanying text.

50. Harkless v. Sweeny Indep. Sch. Dist., 554 F.2d 1353 (5th Cir. 1977), *cert. denied*, 434 U.S. 966 (1977); United States v. Texas Educ. Agency, 459 F.2d 600 (5th Cir. 1972); *cf.* Clark v. Mann, 562 F.2d 1104 (8th Cir. 1977). In the only pertinent published decision under state law, the plaintiff teacher won reinstatement but with reevaluation rather than with tenure. Guilderland Cent. Sch. Dist. v. New York State Human Rights Appeals Bd., 461 N.Y.S.2d 599 (App. Div. 1983).

51. Smith v. Denver Pub. Sch. Bd., 1994 U.S. App. LEXIS 32715 (10th Cir. 1994); Patterson v. Masem, 774 F.2d 251 (8th Cir. 1985); Love v. Alamance County Bd. of Educ., 757 F.2d 1504 (4th Cir. 1985); Jones v. Jefferson Parish Sch. Bd., 533 F. Supp. 816 (E.D. La. 1982), *aff'd mem.*, 688 F.2d 837 (5th Cir. 1982), *cert. denied*, 460 U.S. 1064 (1983); Thompson v. School Dist., 623 F.2d 46 (8th Cir. 1980); Evans v. School Dist., 861 F. Supp. 851 (W.D. Mo. 1994); Love v. Special Sch. Dist., 606 F. Supp. 1320 (E.D. Mo. 1985); *cf.* Harris v. Board of Educ., 798 F. Supp. 1331 (S.D. Ohio 1992) (race discrimination largely but not entirely dismissed); Sklenar v. Central Bd. of Educ., 497 F. Supp. 1154 (E.D. Mich. 1980) (national origin discrimination). *But cf.* Hemmige v. Chicago Pub. Sch.,

786 F.2d 280 (7th Cir. 1986) (national origin discrimination). In *Evans,* the plaintiff prevailed on a separable Title VII claim of retaliation.

52. *See, e.g.,* Verniero v. Air Force Acad. Sch. Dist., 705 F.2d 388 (10th Cir. 1983); Harris v. Board of Educ., 798 F. Supp. 1331 (S.D. Ohio 1992); Danzl v. North St. Paul-Maplewood-Oakdale Indep. Sch. Dist., 663 F.2d 65 (8th Cir. 1981); Zink v. Board of Educ, 497 N.E.2d 835 (Ill. App. Ct. 1986); Stone v. Belgrade Sch. Dist., 703 P.2d 136 (Mont. 1985). *But see* Tye v. Houston County Dist. Bd. of Educ., 681 F. Supp. 740 (M.D. Ala. 1987); Civil Rights Div. v. Amphitheater Unified Sch. Dist., 680 P.2d 517 (Ariz. Ct. App. 1983).

53. *See, e.g.,* Wood v. Omaha Sch. Dist., 25 F.3d 667 (8th Cir. 1994); Cadelli v. Fort Smith Sch. Dist., 23 F.3d 1295 (8th Cir. 1994); Byrne v. Board of Educ., 979 F.2d 560 (7th Cir. 1992); Tafoya v. Bobroff, 865 F. Supp. 742 (D.N.M. 1994); Harris v. Board of Educ., 798 F. Supp. 1331 (S.D. Ohio 1992); Pendleton v. Jefferson Local Sch. Dist., 754 F. Supp. 570 (S.D. Ohio 1990). *But see* Recanzone v. Washoe County Sch. Dist., 696 F. Supp. 1372 (Nev. 1988). For an overview, see Margaret McMenamin and Perry Zirkel, "A Legal Primer on Disability Discrimination in Public School Employment," *Journal of School Leadership* (in press). For a case that illustrates the relationship between reasonable accommodation, which is required, and "normal evaluation procedures," which appear to be unimpeded, *see* Borkowski v. Valley Cent. Sch. Dist., 63 F.3d 132 (2d Cir. 1995).

54. A possibly emerging additional civil rights category is age, based on the Age Discrimination in Employment Act. For a recent and relevant age-discrimination ruling, in which the court rejected summary judgment for the school district, see Sekor v. Capwell, 889 F. Supp. 34 (D. Conn. 1995).

55. *See, e.g.,* Connick v. Myers, 401 U.S. 138 (1983); Mt. Healthy v. Doyle, 429 U.S. 274 (1983); *see also* Perry Zirkel, ed., *NOLPE Case Citations 16: How Free Is Speech in the Schools* (Topeka, Kans.: National Organization on Legal Problems of Education, 1994).

56. *See, e.g.*, Cox v. Dardanelle Pub. Sch. Dist., 790 F.2d 668 (8th Cir. 1986); Hinkle v. Christensen, 733 F.2d 74 (8th Cir. 1984); Hickman v. Valley Local Sch. Dist. Bd. of Educ., 619 F.2d 606 (6th Cir. 1980); Eckerd v. Indian River Sch. Dist., 475 F. Supp. 1350 (D. Del. 1979); *cf.* Kessler v. Monsour, 865 F. Supp. 234 (M.D. Pa. 1994).

57. *See, e.g.*, Cliff v. Board of Sch. Comm'rs, 42 F.3d 403 (7th Cir. 1994); Cromley v. Board of Educ., 17 F.3d 1059 (7th Cir. 1994), *cert. denied*, 115 S. Ct. 74 (1994); Knapp v. Whitaker, 757 F.2d 827 (7th Cir. 1985), *cert. denied*, 474 U.S. 803 (1985); Ifill v. District of Columbia, 665 A.2d 185 (D.C. App. 1995); *cf.* Sekor v. Capwell, 889 F. Supp. 34 (D. Conn. 1995) (lack of threshold prerequisites for administrator and board liability); Board of Educ. v. Illinois Educ. Labor Relations Bd., 616 N.E.2d 1281 (Ill. App. Ct. 1993) (unprotected activity under state collective bargaining statute).

58. *See, e.g.*, Knarr v. Board of Sch. Trustees, 452 F.2d 649 (7th Cir. 1972); *cf.* Board of Trustees v. Gates, 461 So.2d 730 (Miss. 1984), *res judicata*, Gates v. Walker, 865 F. Supp. 1222 (S.D. Miss. 1994).

59. *See, e.g.*, Needleman v. Bohlen, 602 F.2d 1 (1st Cir. 1979); Derrickson v. Board of Educ., 537 F. Supp. 338 (E.D. Mo. 1980); Foreman v. Vermilion Parish Sch. Bd., 353 So.2d 471 (La. Ct. App. 1977).

60. Roberts v. Houston Indep. Sch. Dist., 788 S.W.2d 107 (Tex. Ct. App. 1990).

61. Johnson v. Francis Howell R-3 Bd. of Educ., 868 S.W.2d 191 (Mo. Ct. App. 1993).

62. *See, e.g.*, Williams v. School Dist., 447 S.W.2d 256 (Mo. 1969); McLaughlin v. Tilendis, 253 N.E.2d 85 (Ill. App. Ct. 1962); *cf.* Agins v. Darmstadter, 544 N.Y.S.2d 635 (1989); Buckner v. Carlton, 623 S.W.2d 102 (Tex. Ct. App. 1981).

63. *See, e.g.*, Manguso v. Oceanside Unified Sch. Dist., 200 Cal. Rptr. 535 (Ct. App. 1984); *cf.* Malia v. Monchak, 543 A.2d 184 (Pa. Commw. Ct. 1988); Goralski v. Pizzimenti, 540 A.2d 595 (Pa. Commw. Ct. 1988); *cf.* Zerr v. Johnson, 894 F. Supp. 372 (D. Colo. 1995). Such a conditional immunity also has been accorded to parents' evaluative statements about teachers. *See, e.g.*, Nodar v. Galbreath, 462 So.2d 803 (Fla. 1985).

64. Grostick v. Ellsworth, 404 N.W.2d 685 (Mich. Ct. App. 1987); *see also* Bego v. Gordon, 407 N.W.2d 801 (S.D. 1987).

65. Supan v. Michelfeld, 468 N.Y.S.2d 384 (App. Div. 1983).

66. Pinion v. Alabama State Tenure Comm'n, 415 So.2d 1091 (Ala. Civ. Ct. App. 1982); Cook v. Plainfield Community Sch. Dist., 301 N.W.2d 771 (Iowa Ct. App. 1980).

67. Sankar v. Detroit Bd. of Educ., 409 N.W.2d 213 (Mich. Ct. App. 1987).

68. Franklin v. Harris, 762 S.W.2d 847 (Mo. Ct. App. 1989).

69. Belcher v. Jefferson County Bd. of Educ., 474 So.2d 1063 (Ala. 1985).

70. *See, e.g.*, Siglin v. Kayenta Unified Sch. Dist., 655 P.2d 353 (Ariz. Ct. App. 1982); Thompson v. Board of Educ., 668 P.2d 954 (Colo. Ct. App. 1983); Beebee v. Haslett Pub. Sch., 278 N.W.2d 37 (Mich. Ct. App. 1979); In re Termination of Johnson, 451 N.W.2d 343 (Minn. Ct. App. 1990); Clarke v. Board of Educ., 482 N.Y.S.2d 80 (App. Div. 1984); *cf.* de Koevend v. Board of Educ., 688 P.2d 219 (Colo. 1984); Parmeter v. Feinberg, 482 N.Y.S.2d 80 (App. Div. 1984). *But cf.* Bourland v. Commission on Professional Competence, 219 Cal. Rptr. 906 (Ct. App. 1985).

71. Mills v. Doyle, 407 So.2d 348 (Fla. 1981).

72. Brogan v. School Comm., 516 N.E.2d 159 (Mass. 1987).

73. Klein Indep. Sch. Dist. v. Mattox, 830 F.2d 576 (5th Cir. 1987), *cert. denied,* 485 U.S. 1008 (1988).

74. Hovet v. Hebron Pub. Sch. Dist., 419 N.W.2d 189 (N.D. 1988).

75. *See, e.g.*, Anchorage Sch. Dist. v. Anchorage Daily News, 779 P.2d 1191 (Alaska 1989); Librach v. Cooper, 778 S.W.2d 351 (Mo. Ct. App. 1989); Bowman v. Parma Bd. of Educ., 542 N.E.2d 663 (Ohio Ct. App. 1989). *But cf.* Booth Newspapers, Inc. v. Kalamazoo Sch. Dist., 450 N.W.2d 286 (Mich. Ct. App. 1989) (identity redacted).

76. *See, e.g.,* Guard Publishing Co. v. Lane County Sch. Dist., 791 P.2d 854 (Or. 1990) (strike replacements' names and addresses); Brouillet v. Cowles Publishing Co., 791 P.2d 516 (Wash. 1990) (revoked teaching certificate).

77. Ottochian v. Freedom of Information Comm'n, 604 A.2d 351 (Conn. 1992).

78. Brown v. Seattle Pub. Sch., 860 P.2d 1059 (Wash. Ct. App. 1993). *app. denied*, 877 P.2d 696 (Wash. 1994).

79. Ollie v. Highland Sch. Dist., 749 P.2d 757 (Wash. Ct. App. 1993).
80. Elentuck v. Green, 608 N.Y.S.2d 701 (App. Div. 1994).

Summary Chart of Legislation, Regulations, and Guidelines

L = legislation
R = regulations
G = guidelines

States	Legislation	Regulation	Guidelines	Board of Education discretion	Superintendent/designee	Principal/supervisor	Other	Teachers and other staff	Teachers only	Non-tenured teachers only	Continuous	Annual	At Intervals	Different for tenured/non-tenured staff	General	Categorical	Formal Instrument	Remediation non-tenured	Remediation tenured	Remedial period non-tenured	Remedial period tenured	Copy	Teacher Test	Other	Comments
AL	✓		1	R				L							L			L	L	L	L	L	L		[1]guidelines state evaluation period, type, and process
AK	✓	✓		2			1		L			R			L			L	L		L	L			[1]any certified administrator; evaluators must be trained
AZ	✓		1	2				L							L	2		L	L	L		L			[2]evaluators must be trained
AR	1		✓		L			L						G	L		L	L	L	L		L			[1]contains instruments
CA	✓						2	L						G		2								1	[2]requires dev. with teacher reps./agents [2]evaluators must be trained
CO	1				2			L			L				L	L						L			[1]student progress
CT	✓		1			L		L			L	L			L	2		L	L	L	L	L			[1]requires dev. with teacher/citizens [1]any certified administrator
DE	1		1			L		L				L			L	L		L	L	L	L	L			[1]guidelines state type and process of eval. [2]bd. dev. with teacher reps.
FL	1	✓	✓		L			L									L	L	L	L	L	L			[1]state policy addresses all five categories
GA	✓		1					L							L		L	L	L	L	L	L			[1]establish institute to dev. teacher eval. [2]supt. establishes procedures
HI	✓	✓					2	L				L			L		L					L			[2]Professional Standards Commission designee
ID	✓		✓					L				L			L							L			[1]policy, in effect, has force of law; LEA is SEA.
IL	✓		1			L								L	L			L	L	L	L	L			[1]requires dev. with teachers/bargaining agent [2]certified administrators
IN	1	✓	2				2							L	L							L			[1]process subject to bargaining [2]guidelines address type and process
IA	1	✓					2								L										[1]evaluation process subject to bargaining [2]licensed evaluators
KS	✓							L								L						L			[1]student performance
KY	✓	✓	1	L			2	L						L	L	R	R								[1]guidelines state who eval. and type [2]cert. eval. or KY "distinguished ed."
LA	✓		1	L				L				L		L	L			L	L	L	L	L			[1]guidelines state type of evaluation and process

32

State	C1	C2	C3	C4	C5	C6	C7	C8	C9	C10	C11	C12	C13	C14	C15	C16	C17	C18	C19	Notes
ME	1			L				L												¹Dept. of Ed. to est. models
MD	✓				L															¹State bd. req. eval.; negotiated agree. common
MA	1				L			L			L	L					L		2	¹subject to collective bargaining ²may include student performance
MI	1			L			L				L				L		L			¹subject to collective bargaining
MN	1			L				L			L	L								¹requires bargaining for tenured teachers ²non-tenured teachers
MS	1			L			L				L	L		L			L		L	¹Dept. of Education assists local districts in establishing
MO	✓	1				L						L		L		L	L			¹guidelines state evaluation process
MT	✓	✓		L			R										R			
NB	✓	✓		L			L				L	L								¹procedures for approval of eval. policy
NV	1						L				L	L		L	L		L			¹requires policy development with teachers' elected reps.
NH		✓		R		R														
NJ	✓	✓		R				L			R	R							1	¹includes pupil "progress and growth"
NM	✓	1				2	L													¹guidelines state who evaluates and type of eval. ²"level III-A teachers"
NY	1			L			L			L										¹requires development with teachers and administrators
NC	✓	1								L		L								¹guidelines state who is to be evaluated, type of evaluation and process
ND	✓						L				L						L			
OH	✓			L			L				L	L		L	L		L			
OK	1			L			L				L		L	L	L	L	L	L	L	¹requires consultation with teachers' representatives; subject to bargain
OR	1				L		L				L	L		L	L		L			¹board establishes policy with teachers' reps or bargaining agent
PA	✓				L		L				L		L	1			R	R		¹alternative must be approved by PA Dept. of Education
RI	1			L																¹subject to collective bargaining
SC	✓			L			L				L	L				L	L	L		
SD	✓	✓		L			L				L		R	L	L		R			
TN	✓					1	L				L		L	L	L					¹"career level III teachers, principals, asst. principals, or superintendents"
TX	✓	1		L					L		L									¹guidelines state type and process of evaluation
UT	1				L					L							L			¹requires dev. by joint comm. of elected teachers/adm. for Board approval
VT	✓	✓				1														¹"local standards board"
VA		1																		¹guidelines address all five categories
WA	1	✓		L	L		L				L	R		L	L	L	L	L	L	¹5 yr+ employees' evaluation may be bargained
WV	✓	1		L			L			G										¹guidelines require employee copy
WI	✓			L			L				L	1								¹based on job descriptions
WY	✓				L		L				L						L			

Summary Chart Citations

For each state, the sequence of sources of information is: 1) legislation, 2) regulations, and 3) related policies and guidelines. The items in the third category are shown in brackets because they do not have the force of law and because the sampling of guidelines in this list is less complete. Legislative citations were compiled through use of the LEXIS database using significators of *tenure, dismissal, evaluation, performance, standards, teacher, educators, professional,* and *development.*

The category, *who evaluates,* is based on who has the responsibility for conducting, or causing to be conducted, evaluations. In almost half the states, the responsibility is delegated to the local board of education or its equivalent, though Arizona and Arkansas require that board-designated evaluators be trained specifically for the task. *Who is evaluated* ranges from teachers and other personnel, required in 26 states, to only teachers, required in Arizona, Maryland, and Minnesota. In addition, Montana prescribes evaluations for nontenured teachers. In 22 states, the *Evaluation period* differs for tenured and nontenured personnel, with the frequency of evaluation greater for nontenured personnel.

Legislative requirements for evaluation range from none in 24 states to a general prescription for some type of process in 20 states to a categorical list of attributes and achievements that are to be considered for performance evaluation. Four states specifically require consideration of student performance, though California proscribes the use of normed student scores on standardized tests as a factor.

Both *Remediation* and *Remedial periods* are required for both tenured and nontenured teachers in seven states. Seven states require remediation for both tenured and nontenured teachers, two states require a remedial period for both tenured and nontenured teachers, and Montana requires both remediation and a remedial period for only nontenured teachers. Remediation ranges from "confer and consult" to a specified written plan. Twenty states specify how evaluation copies are to be handled, generally requiring that a copy of the evaluation be provided within a specified time to the person who was evaluated.

Finally, a broad caveat is warranted. The specific language and contextual location of the relevant statutes and regulations vary considerably; their placement into the selected categories of this brief chart is subject to interpretation. For example, the boundaries between teacher evaluation for dismissal, which is the focus of this chart, and teacher assessment for certification or recertification, which is not included in the chart, are not always clear cut. Moreover, these laws are subject to change.

The compiler of this chart wishes to thank Dr. Sandra Tracy, who provided many of the policy and guidelines documents.

Alabama
1991 Ala. Acts 459; ALA. CODE Sec. 16-23-16.1
[Alabama State Department of Education. State Plan for Inservice Education/Professional Development.]

Alaska
ALASKA STAT. Secs. 14.20.450 and 14.20.480
ALASKA ADMIN. CODE tit. 4 Chapter 19

Arizona
ARIZ. REV. STAT. ANN. Secs. 15-537 and 15-538
[Department of Education. Qualified Evaluator Training Manual Arizona.]

Arkansas
ARK. STAT. ANN. Secs. 6-17-201, 6-17-202, 6-17-203, and 6-17-1504
[Arkansas Department of Education. Arkansas Evaluation Sub-Committee Report (December 1984).]

California
CAL. EDUC. CODE Secs. 44660-44664 and 44938

Colorado
COLO. REV. STAT. Secs. 22-9-l02, 22-9-103, 22-9-104, 22-9-106, and 22-9-107
[Colorado Department of Education. Certificated Personnel Performance Evaluation Act Guidelines (February 1991).]

Connecticut
CONN. GEN. STAT. Sec. 10-151b, 10-155c, and 10-220a
[Connecticut State Department of Education. Guidelines for Comprehensive Professional Development Plans (1990).]
[Connecticut State Department of Education. The Fifteen Connecticut Teacher Competencies: Standards and Procedures for Approval of Teacher Preparation Programs (1984).]

Delaware
[Delaware State Board of Education. Policy for Appraising Teachers and Specialists (1990).]

Florida
FLA. STAT. ANN. Secs. 231.29 and 231.65
State Bd. of Educ. Rules 6A-4.046, 6A-5.057, and 6A-5.061
[Florida Department of Education. Handbook for the Review of District Instructional Personnel Assessment Systems (1988).]

Georgia
GA. CODE ANN. Secs. 20-2-200, 20-2-210, and 20-2-230
[Georgia Department of Education. Georgia Teacher Evaluation Program (1989).]

Hawaii

(*See also* Hawaii Senate Resolution (SR) 32.)
HAW. REV. STAT. Sec. 297-46
[Department of Education. Program for Assessing Teaching in Hawaii: Manual for Evaluators and Participants (1993).]

Idaho

IDAHO CODE Secs. 33-514, 33-515, and 33-517
IDAHO ADMIN. CODE Sec. 08.02.C.35

Illinois

ILL. REV. STAT. ch. 105, para. 24A-1 et seq.
ILL. ADMIN. CODE Secs. 50.20, 50.30, 50.40, 50.50, and 50.55

Indiana

IND. CODE Sec. 20-6.1-9
[Indiana Department of Education. Staff Performance Evaluation.]

Iowa

IOWA CODE Secs. 260.33, 272.1, 272.33, and 279.14
IOWA ADMIN. CODE r. 12.3(4)

Kansas

KAN. STAT. ANN. Secs. 72-9003, 72-9004, and 72-9005

Kentucky

KY. REV. STAT. ANN. Sec. 156.101 and 161.790
704 KY. ADMIN. REGS. 3:345
[Kentucky Department of Education. Teacher/Administrator Performance Based Evaluation: Guidelines for Certified Personnel Evaluation.]

Louisiana

LA. REV. STAT. ANN. Sec. 17:3902 and 17:3904

Maine

ME. REV. STAT. ANN. tit. 20-A, Sec. 13802
Me. Code R. Sec. 4.2

Maryland
MD. CODE ANN., EDUC. Secs. 4-205 and 6-103

Massachusetts
MASS. ANN. LAWS ch. 71, Sec. 38

Michigan
MICH. STAT. ANN. Secs. 15.1983, 15.1983(1), and 15.1993

Minnesota
MINN. STAT. Secs. 125.2 and 125.12

Mississippi
MISS. CODE ANN. Secs. 37-3-2 and 37-3-46

Missouri
MO. REV. STAT. Secs. 168.114, 168.116, 168.128, and 168.410
[Missouri Department of Elementary and Secondary Education.
Guidelines for Performance Based Evaluation (1991).]

Montana
MONT. CODE ANN. Secs. 20-4-402 and 20-4-403
MONT. ADMIN. R. 10.55.701

Nebraska
NEB. REV. STAT. Secs 79-328(5) (I) and 79-12,111
NEB. ADMIN. R. & REGS. Tit 92, ch. 34

Nevada
NEV. REV. STAT. ANN. Secs 391.312, 391.3125, 391.3127, and
319.313

New Hampshire
N.H. CODE ADMIN. R. EDUC. Secs. 302.02 and 304.01

New Jersey
N.J. STAT. ANN. Sec. 18A:27-3.1
N.J. ADMIN. CODE tit. 6, Secs. 6:3-1.9, 6:3-1.21, and 6:11-3.4

New Mexico
N.M. STAT. ANN. Secs. 22-10-3.1 and 22-10-21
[State Board of Education. Competencies for Educational Personnel.]

New York
N.Y. EDUC LAW Sec. 100.2

North Carolina
1979 N.C. Sess. Laws Sec. 35

North Dakota
N.D. CENT. Code Secs. 15-47-26, 15-47-27, and 15-47-27.1

Ohio
OHIO REV. CODE ANN. Secs. 3319.01, 3319.02, and 3319.111

Oklahoma
70 OKLA. STAT. ANN. Secs. 6-101.11, 6-101.21, 6-101.24, and 6-103.2

Oregon
OR. REV. STAT. Sec. 342.850

Pennsylvania
24 PA. STAT. ANN. Secs. 11-1108 and 11-1123
22 PA. CODE Secs. 351.21-351.26

Rhode Island
R.I. GEN. LAWS Sec. 16-2-9

South Carolina
S. C. CODE ANN. Sec. 59-25-440, 59-26-10, 59-26-30, and 59-26-40

South Dakota
S.D. CODIFIED LAWS Sec. 13-43-9.1
S.D. ADMIN. R. 24:08:05, App. A

Tennessee

TENN. CODE ANN. Secs. 49-5-5204 and 49-5-5205

Texas

TEX. EDUC. CODE ANN. Sec. 21.202
[Texas Education Agency. Texas Teacher Appraisal System.]

Utah

UTAH CODE ANN. Secs. 53A-10-103, 53A-10-104, 53A-10-106, 53A-10-107, 53A-10-108, and 53A-10-109

Vermont

[State Board of Education. Professional Standards: Defining, Enacting and Putting Them into Practice.]

Virginia

[Virginia Department of Education. Resource Book for Teacher Evaluation.]

Washington

WASH. REV. CODE Sec. 28A.405.100

West Virginia

W. VA. CODE Secs. 18A-2-8, 18A-2-12, and 18A-3A-2
W. VA. Bd. of Educ. Policy No. 5300 (6) (d)

Wisconsin

WIS. STAT. Sec. 121.02

Wyoming

WYO. STAT. Sec. 21-3-110 and 21-3-111

Resources

Beckham, Joseph. *Legal Aspects of Teacher Evaluation*. Topeka, Kans.: National Organization on Legal Problems of Education, 1981.

Beckham, Joseph. *Legal Aspects of Employee Assessment and Selection*. Topeka, Kans.: National Organization on Legal Problems of Education, 1985.

Beckham, Joseph. "Legally Sound Criteria: Processes and Procedures for the Evaluation of Public School Professional Employees." *Journal of Law & Education* 14 (1985): 529-52.

Citron, Christiana. "An Overview of Legal Issues in Teacher Quality." *Journal of Law & Education* 14 (1985): 277-308.

Claxton, William. "Remediation: The Evolving Fairness in Teacher Dismissal." *Journal of Law & Education* 15 (1986): 181-94.

Clear, Delbert, and Box, John. "Justifiable Performance Standards for Discharging Incompetent Teachers." In *School Law Update 1985*, edited by T. Jones and D. Semler. Topeka, Kans.: National Organization on Legal Problems of Education, 1985.

DeMitchell, Todd. "Competence, Documentation, and Dismissal: A Legal Template." *International Journal of Educational Reform* 4 (1995): 88-95.

Frase, Larry, and Downey, Carolyn. "Teacher Dismissal: Crucial Substantive Due Process Guidelines from Court Cases." *National Forum of Applied Educational Research* 4 (1990-91): 13.

Frase, Larry, and Downey, Carolyn. "Teacher Dismissal: Crucial Procedural Due Process Guidelines from Court Cases." *National Forum of Applied Educational Research* 4 (1991-92): 17-23.

Frels, Kelly, and Cooper, Timothy. "Documentation of Employee Performance." In *Legal Issues in Public School Employment*, edited by Joseph Beckham and Perry A. Zirkel. Bloomington, Ind.: Phi Delta Kappa, 1983.

Hazi, Helen, and Garman, Noreen. "Legalizing Scientism Through Teacher Evaluation." *Journal of Personnel Evaluation in Education* 2 (1988): 7-18.

Holley, William, and Feild, Hubert. "The Law and Performance Evaluation in Education." *Journal of Law & Education* 6 (1977): 427-48.

Menacker, Julius. "A Dilemma in Teacher Dismissal Hearings." *West's Education Law Reporter* 93 (1994): 459-69.

Jascourt, Hugh; Rynecki, Steven; Lindquist, John; and Zerger, Kirsten. "Teacher Evaluation and Collective Bargaining." *Journal of Law & Education* 17 (1988): 485-526.

Peterson, Donovan. "Legal and Ethical Issues of Teacher Evaluation." *Educational Research Quarterly* 7 (1983): 6-16.

Petrie, Bruce, and Black, Timothy. "Termination in Ohio for 'Gross Inefficiency': The Role of Teacher Evaluation." *Ohio State Law Journal* 44 (1983): 1041-50.

Pope, Laura Means. "State Regulation of Educator Evaluation." In *Legal Issues in Public School Employment*, edited by Joseph Beckham and Perry A. Zirkel. Bloomington, Ind.: Phi Delta Kappa, 1983.

Rebell, Michael. "Teacher Performance Assessment: The Changing State of the Law." *Journal of Personnel Evaluation in Education* 5 (1991): 227-35.

Rossow, Lawrence, and Parkinson, Jerry. *The Law of Teacher Evaluation*. Topeka, Kans.: National Organization on Legal Problems of Education, 1992.

Shaw, Frank. "A Summary of Legal Implications of Teacher Evaluations for Merit Pay and a Model Plan." *Educational Administration Quarterly* 21 (1985): 51-69.

Sperry, David; Pounder, Diana; and Drew, Clifford. "Educator Evaluation and the Law: A Case Study." *West's Education Law Reporter* 75 (1992): 965-79.

Valentine, Jerry W. *Principles and Practices for Effective Teacher Evaluation*. Boston: Allyn & Bacon, 1992.

Zirkel, Perry A. "Evaluating Teacher Effectiveness: A Legal Perspective." *Action in Teacher Education* 2 (1979-80): 17-25.

Appendix

Those readers who might have been surprised at their scores on the self-assessment on pages 4-5 may want to compare their scores to those of the participants at Harvard's Institute on School Law who took the pilot version of the assessment in the summers of 1994 and 1995. Most of those participants had above-average knowledge of legal issues in education, and they had shown sufficient interest in legal issues to enroll in and travel to the institute from various parts of the country. About 55% were superintendents; 20% were principals and supervisors; 15% were university faculty or administrators; and 5% were attorneys. The respondents to the pilot version of the assessment had, on average, 20 years of professional experience; and approximately 60% had taken at least two graduate course in education law, while another 30% had taken one graduate course in education law. The distribution of answers from the 75 participants were:

Item	A	B	C	D	E	NR	
1. Test scores	21%	27%	11%	19%	21%	1%	(73% incorrect)
2. Negotiability/ Arbitrability	24%	15%	9%	33%	17%	1%	(61% incorrect)
3. Remediation	12%	7%	8%	31%	41%	1%	(92% incorrect)
4. Statutory noncompliance	9%	9%	8%	31%	39%	4%	(92% incorrect)
5. Local policy noncompliance			* * * [not included in pilot-testing draft] * * *				

6. Subjective criteria	15%	24%	23%	20%	16%	3%	(85% incorrect)
7. Discrimination	13%	16%	21%	29%	15%	5%	(56% incorrect)
8. Outspokenness	12%	19%	24%	23%	17%	5%	(81% incorrect)
9. Videotaping	3%	13%	11%	17%	55%	1%	(84% incorrect)
10. Defamation	13%	20%	11%	24%	27%	5%	(87% incorrect)
11. Other costly consequences	1%	7%	15%	28%	49%	0%	(93% incorrect)
12. Insubordination	3%	5%	8%	43%	39%	3%	(61% incorrect)
13. Open records legislation	5%	9%	4%	24%	55%	3%	(87% incorrect)

Overall, this above-average group selected the correct responses only 21% of the time. If there was only one correct answer to each question, then 20% would be the score one could expect from chance, or just randomly guessing at the answers. Because many of the items have two possible correct answers, these participants scored significantly less than chance. While some of these participants may have been accurately reflecting their local regulations, it is more likely that their answers represented the "lore" of teacher evaluation, not the law.

The items where the answers were particularly skewed toward the lore and not the law were numbers 3 (remediation), 4 (statutory compliance), 6 (subjectivity), 10 (defamation), 11 (other costly consequences), and 13 (open records).

About the Author

Perry A. Zirkel is University Professor of Education and Law at Lehigh University, where he formerly was dean of the College of Education. He has a Ph.D. in Educational Administration, a J.D. from the University of Connecticut, and a Master of Laws degree from Yale University.

Zirkel has written more than 200 publications on school law. He is the author, with Sharon Nalbone Richardson and Steven S. Goldberg, of *A Digest of Supreme Court Decisions Affecting Education, Third Edition*, published by Phi Delta Kappa in 1995. Zirkel developed the first edition of the *Digest* in 1978. He also is the co-editor, with Joseph Beckham, of *Legal Issues in Public School Employment*, published by Phi Delta Kappa in 1983. Zirkel writes a regular column on legal issues in education, called "Courtside," for the *Phi Delta Kappan* journal, as well as a regular column published jointly in *Principal* and *NASSP Bulletin*.

He is an active labor arbitrator and also serves on the special education hearing appeals panel for Pennsylvania. Zirkel is the current president of the National Organization on Legal Problems of Education (NOLPE), which has headquarters in Topeka, Kansas.